Of Deserts & Rivers

FIRST EDITION 2004
10 9 8 7 6 5 4 3 2 1

LIBRARY OF CONGRESS CATALOG CARD NUMBER: 2004 115641
ISBN: 0–938631–31–4 paper

BOOK DESIGN/PRODUCTION: V. S. Elliott, SunFlower Designs of Santa Fe
TYPEFACE: Bernhard Modern, Pompeia Inline, Mona Lisa Solid

PUBLISHED BY:

ᑭ PENNYWHISTLE PRESS
PO Box 734
Tesuque, New Mexico 87574
pennywhistlebook@aol.com

To Patricia,
who has been part of
my life for so many
years and through so
many "vicissitudes"
(beautiful or not)!
Love,
Annamaria
February 05

Of Deserts & Rivers

Annamaria de Nicolais Napolitano

Not Marble, nor the gilded monuments
Of Princes, shall outlive this powerful rhyme;
But you shall shine more bright in these contents
Than unswept stone besmear'd with sluttish time.

WILLIAM SHAKESPEARE

Hay una raiz amarga
Y un mundo de mil terrazas.

There is a bitter root
And a world of a thousand terraces.

¡Amor, enemigo mio,
Muerde tu raiz amarga!

Love, my foe,
Bite your bitter root!

FEDERICO GARCIA LORCA
Gacela de La Raiz Amarga

To Mario who walks with me on sand, on water
and with me rides the stars

ANNAMARIA

CONTENTS

Measuring up to the pyramids in Giza, Egypt.

The Author In The Desert...

Annamaria Napolitano née de Nicolais, was born in Naples in a close-knit family, with all the psychological and social constrictions and problems of a nobility, by now poor and decayed, of the old Italian south. This was a life based on an oppressive morality, a lifestyle founded on old outmoded principles, an excessive Catholicism, polarized by two irreconcilable political realities: loyalty to the still-potent monarchic ideal on the one hand, and, on the other, the republican tradition inherited, on the maternal side, from Luigi Settembrini, the Author's grandfather, famous in the annals of Neapolitan history as the uncompromising follower of Mazzini. On the paternal side there was an equally illustrious name, that of the Davalos D'Aragona d'Acquaviva, Spanish nobles who, 600 years before, were induced, by political necessities, to seek refuge in Benevento, a little town not far from Naples. Strict obedience, uncompromising morality, unforgiving intransigence, and the faint surviving echoes of ancient pride inform the early familiar life of our Author.

1

Her childhood is forever marked by the atrocities of the Second World War, to which she is an unwilling, uncomprehending spectator, perennially frightened, perennially on the edge of hunger, surviving on a barely-adequate diet. Her earliest memories include the full tremendous cacophony of war: alarms, aerial bombardments, uncertain safety in comfortless but somehow comforting shelters. She is a minuscule particle buffeted by a sea of desperate humanity hunting for the illusion of safety amid the roar of falling bombs against a backdrop of ruin and destruction, while the ground itself heaves and shakes in impotent protest. The sense of powerlessness and of tenuous safety within the protection of a layer of humanity sharing the same fate is explicitly captured in *Italy First Love*, one of the poems in *To Know the Desert*, previously published in the anthology *Sextet One:*

The dawn of death on	*always*
The sound of life within	*always*
The smell of love beneath	*always*
The mystery of fate around	*always*
The labor of life close	*always*
To belong finally	
To the familial bond	*always*

Her family is subject to all the indignities of the German occupation, and she is a witness to the harrowing escapes just managed by her father, her uncle, her grandfather, all in constant danger of capture and imprisonment, or worse, by the occupiers. It is these Germans who are by now engaged in a last futile and vengeful struggle against the irresistible advance of the Allies and against the "traitorous" Italians. Even though too young to comprehend the immanent, ever-present danger, she senses the terror of the adults, internalizes and amplifies it and is dominated and shaped by it.

The war over, the family settles slowly into a more normal routine, and the child author begins to live a normal child's life. She is enrolled in a prestigious school for the daughters of prominent Neapolitan families, the same school in which her aunt and her mother have studied, and whose director had been a childhood friend of her maternal grandmother, Nobil Donna Chiara Capuano Settembrini. This is a confusing time in Annamaria's life, full of conflicting messages: on the one hand, expectations and ritualistic ostentation of wealth and influence, on the other, the lack of material means to support such expectations. But she thrives in school, loves to study and to read. She grows alone, the only girl-child in a family of adults, floating on a sea of books that fill her head with exotic ideas and induct her into a world of fantasy and unbridled imagination. She begins to feel, confusedly, the restrictions imposed on her, in the "real" world, by her femaleness. A constant litany, she can't do this or that because she "is little, and a girl". She dreams of being a man, roaming free and wild across the oceans of the world, alone if necessary. Again, she writes it down in haunting fashion in *Today I Smelled the Sea*, part of the present collection:

> *Then, in resplendent solitude,*
> *I rode a wooden horse into the horizon*
> *Raced the elusive brothers below the keel...*
> *I was the sun child: my hair turned to gold,*
> *The salt on my skin gave wings to my flight*
> *The sky was close and the stars were mine.*

I counted them one by one,
At dawn, I stole the brightest and wore it on my chest…
Mother questioned the gift,
I lied and said "God's"

Here we see the ambivalence, the desire for derring-do, but also the craving for approval, the wish to be a "good" girl. Annamaria's poetry is always intensely personal, but, through the universality of her personal experiences, she reaches out to the immanent humanity in all of us. She is eminently human in that there is nothing abstract in her drive to flight; she particularizes and concretizes. Having read Salgari, she wants to be a pirate, or at least Jolanda, the daughter of the Black Corsair, for Jolanda wears pants, a practice absolutely forbidden by Annamaria's mother, who considers it symptomatic of a looseness and liberality totally at odds with the decorum and dignity of the family. Annamaria dreams of wearing pants and of having incredible adventures in exotic places: she lives in a surreal world that replaces the unsatisfying world of everyday life.

At the tender age of seven, she is seduced and initiated into the practices of sex by a much older boy who will hold psychological ascendancy over her for years to come. This awakens and nurtures in her a disproportionate inclination towards an enveloping eroticism that marks her for life and determines much of its future course. The experience resonates in her plaintive *Paths:*

It was no time to be a child,
Her tutelage was of a different nature,
Fear stilled her play and hungry mouths devoured her age.
The odd year seven saw her innocence bloom in shame
And pointed the way to things to come,

Legends roamed the sky, yet she walked in sand,
Wore ribbons in her hair and braided her heart.

Not entirely coincidentally, she starts to write at about this time, filling entire notebooks with thoughts, words, poetry. At the age of seventeen she completes the Liceo, graduating first in her class, recipient of a prestigious prize, the responsibility of teaching, in the same school, a kindergarten class. Thus she takes her first tentative steps on what is to became her second lifelong vocation.

She begins her university studies and completes them in the space of three years, taking her major in English Language and Literature. To this she adds a degree, a year later, in European Institutions. At the age of 18 she wins a state competition for aspiring teachers, at the age of 23 she is given her first assignment, teaching English in the Licei the Italian equivalent of high school. She embarks on a teaching career, but "real" life is about to take its revenge on her: she is about to live some of the adventure and intrigue she has longed for these many past years.

Free at last of the incubus of her mentor, she meets, at the age of 20, the man who is to become her husband. But he is already married and 18 years her senior. He falls hopelessly in love with her, proposes picaresque escapades to Marrakech, to Rio, leaves wife and children for her. The scandal spreads, there is only one way out. They leave for America, for a California that to them is little more than a myth, he first, with Annamaria following. It is a country of dream, mysterious and incomprehensible to her, profoundly rooted as she is, in the traditions and customs of life in southern Italy. The trepidation is apparent in *Awakenings (To Know the Desert):*

Smooth, impassible highways
Snaked through the mountains
Consigning magenta hues
To scattered dwellings
Suited to children's ancestral memories.
There, at the intersection,
The womb split and received
The reluctant exile.

Her life is hard, based as it is on the bedrock of her love for this man for whom she has crossed the Ocean. She suffers the separation from her family, especially from her adored mother, she desperately longs for the colors and the smells of her childhood, for the air of her beloved Naples. And she writes, reams and reams, but does not dare to show her writings to anyone, terrified of a judgment that perhaps would serve to stop her in her tracks and take her away forever from pen and paper.

With care and perseverance she learns the language of her new country, learns it well. And, after a couple of years of inconsequential and banal stints in forgotten offices peopled by simple people scornful of her exoticism, she lands a job as a professor in a local college. Shortly thereafter, with renewed self confidence, she knocks on the doors of Stanford University, which open magically for her. With this she embarks on a career that will last 30 years and will bring her to the front ranks as an exponent of Italian language and culture in the Bay Area. She writes a successful *Manuale di Grammatica Italiana*, still used by several schools all over the world. She continues to produce poetry, but in secret, still ashamed of sharing those feelings, become words, with the rest of the world.

She lives through the feminist liberation of the sixties and seventies in a contradictory and confused limbo, with periods of reckless abandon and wanton experimentation, desiring a revolution that she feels just and necessary, but at odds with the conservatism of her upbringing, which has saddled her with deep and long-lasting inhibitions. Her husband is her ballast, imposing a lifestyle more sedate and conservative than her natural inclinations would lead her to investigate. There will always be these two painfully opposing currents in her life: her feeling of belonging to a solidly conservative past, exemplified by the world of "adults" (because, at bottom, she will always feel herself to be a little girl), and her wild drive toward the unknown, the new, the unforeseen adventure.

The death of her husband, her second painful and terrifying emancipation, infuses in her a new maturity and self confidence, so that, when a friend stumbles by accident across some of her writings and urges her to publish, she acquiesces. In this way her first collection of poetry, *To Know the Desert,* is published as part of the anthology *Sextet One.*

To the answer, why and how do you write, her reply is a terse "I don't know." Images and words of irresistible authority rise in her, and they find their way on paper as if by magic, while she is in a state of febrile creativity, outside of herself, and unaware of any conscious effort to invent or structure. She emerges from these bouts exhausted and emotionally drained, reads what she has written, and does not know how it came to be. The creative process is for her a transition to "non-being" or to "being elsewhere", a form of catharsis into which she gets lost, only to find herself again at the end of it. In her disturbing *Rage* she gives flesh to the process, and its inevitability, in near anatomical terms:

Caught, we circle the narrow space
With eyes of flame
And rarely rest in quiet corners

The raised limb reveals the rage
Which ate the flesh at the bone
And exposed the ruptured tendons

Caught, we gaze at the opening
With hearts of lead
And long for the searing pain of living

The themes that recur in her poetry are the essential solitude of the feminine (hence the desert metaphor), the ineffable nostalgia for all the time come and gone, forever lost, for all the might-have-beens, irretrievably gone. Annamaria's past is not necessarily a "better" time, it is simply "another" time, a time that will never repeat, for good or ill. The sense of the passage of time is captured in *Harvest House* through that most ancient and fundamental of clocks, the unrolling of the seasons, and that most common of metaphors, running water:

The spring rolled in with hurried speed,
—And the acquiescence of death —
Broke the stream in a thousand scintillating visions,
Gave the measure of the seasons' ending game:
We no longer visit the marketplace,
We play solitaire, now, in front of a mute screen,
We escalate in a terminal direction.

Then, when the harvest was ripe
We locked the gates,

Then, when the harvest was rich,
We sang the night,
Then, when the harvest was ours,
We dreamt the morning.

The great caravan of life progresses inexorably to an apocalyptic end, loaded with life's suffering and joy. In it there are blue men of strength, nobility, and inner beauty, there are sibyls of mythical powers, and there are simply people. Annamaria is not reticent. In *When the Desert was a River...* she tells us:

Caravans
Led by blue men
...
The fortuneteller sits in the shade
...

but, as always, the fortuneteller is more than what she seems:

She soars in slow, silent circles
Above tired flesh
Consumed, consuming, consummated
She senses the water, she smells it,
Her probable sons used to bathe in it.

The autobiographical element is always very strong in Annamaria's poetry, perhaps even when she does not intend it to be.

The death of her husband provokes two apparently contrasting reactions: on the one hand, sudden freedom from a sick bed that has dominated her life for seven years; on the other, a sense of deep loss and desolation. It is necessary for her to learn to live alone, she who had passed directly from her father to her husband, always directed and managed by others. Her next two years are a mélange of meaningless and directionless events and relationships: she is close to suicide. She is saved by a marvelous voyage to Egypt, during which everything comes together, the enchantment of the land, the Pyramids, the simplicity and sweetness of the people, the sand of a desert no longer merely imagined, the Nile flowing majestically past Aswan. All this works to revive her old wandering fantasies and restore in her a desire to live. Not least, she finds love on the Nile with an innocent northerner: it would have been enough! In *Perhaps* she recounts the experience:

> *You came with light*
> *With sound*
> *With night*
> *You came*
>
> *You came across land*
> *Across water*
> *Across air*
> *You came*
> *You were unforeseen*
>
> *At dawn we parted with a promise*
> *We kept by chance fulfilled*

As is her wont, she launches herself into this new love with every molecule of her being; they spend incredibly romantic interludes in northern Africa, Italy, Germany. It is in this latter country, in Heidelberg, inexplicably far from the sun and warmth of her beloved south, that she learns German, but, more importantly, she slowly learns to live alone.

The new peace that she has found is apparent in *Policastro:*

At peace, away, far,
Anxiety forgotten
And violence with it.

...

The noise of man comes distant
Stays on the threshold, without invading.
Time is no longer a measure
Nobody knocks, not even a memory.

And she needs this knowledge, for this too turns out to be ephemeral and unsatisfying. Her lover is married and unable to break the bonds. She learns to enjoy her solitude and her "freedom", never losing her desire for a family. She sublimates her needs by substituting a network of friends whom she frequents assiduously: they become her "family". This is a period of extensive travel: the Pacific, Africa. She discovers the pleasure of traveling alone, and she writes, wherever she goes, poems, thoughts, travel notes. Her restlessness is evident in the refrain in *Requiem II*

Let us go, let us go, You and I

which betrays her true feelings about her solitary travels.

In 1994 she meets the man who will become her companion: a man of her land, of her city, of her age. In him she rediscovers her tongue, her dialect, long-forgotten idioms, half-remembered songs from her Italian childhood, tastes and smells of long ago. As she writes in *With my People:*

In you, with you
I live ancient memories:
— Smell of new wine

...

— Color of hoarse voices
...

Burning fireplace
Smoke in our hair
Black cauldron
Hot cinders' dust
White roasting tubers
Black aprons
Bowls filled with warm milk
Braids woven with magic
Solemn tales
Dark nocturnal fears

She comes face to face, in effect, with her own history. After a lukewarm beginning (because she is still distracted by the recently concluded love affair), she falls deeply in love with him and dedicates herself to him completely. Unfortunately he declines to reciprocate, so that even this comes with its share of suffering. Her plaintive lament in *Where am I* is the universal cry of all women:

Am I the dawn or the sunset?
Am I the middle of the day or dusk?
Am I a button on your shirt,
The lace in your shoe,
The water for your camel?
...

Where am I in your life?
Whisper it, but say it.

A renewed desire to write possesses her: in 1996 her first collection of poems is published and she begins to write prose. It takes her a single summer to finish a short semi-autobiographical novel, UNA VITA PER CASO, in Italian; she then starts on another novel, also in Italian, L'UOMO DI LIBETRA, and completes it in six months. In a frenzy of creativity, she continues to write an important group of poems that serve as the core of the present anthology in a continuous and caring productive effort.

Annamaria Napolitano is at present still at Stanford University and continues to work, in collaboration with her partner, on another novel, *Appetites,* this time in English.

MARIO FUSCO
Woodside, California

Introduction

In the western tradition, the *Song of Songs* has set the standard for love poetry for centuries. Annamaria Napolitano's poetry alludes to some of the same accessories, pomegranates, figs and the metaphoric enclosed garden, which she describes as the "lover's cocoon." But time enters into the lives of her lovers, who live in the modern world, regardless of their yearning to shut it out, and that world intrudes into the lover's universe, with business, breakfast (where "frowns are most virulent"), and the occasional flash of rage. Hers are mortal lovers, who know that the Song of Solomon, with the promise of a "love stronger than death," is the shattered illusion of those who are no longer young.

Her lovers find their enclosed garden within; outside there is time and the caravan. Perhaps the desert through which it plods has a beauty of which the biblical lovers were unaware, caught up as they were in the mysteries of their newly discovered bodies. There is no hint that they will ever discover it, since they live in a time out of time. For them, the desert was only the space of absence, punctuating the oases of their passion. Napolitano's lovers know there is no space in the trackless desert and that they will not know the destination of their caravans until they arrive, at which time there will be nothing left to know. Their solace, for the moment, is that they are travelling together and that the pain that they must endure (sometimes alternately, sometimes together) makes their love and their pleasure ever more intense.

The Bible too has its desert, but it is the desert of Exodus, the passage between bondage in Egypt and the Promised Land. It was led by Moses, who never reached the goal, and it lasted for forty years. St. Paul read into that tribal epic his own spiritual auto-biography: "I was in bondage for forty years." There is perhaps in Annamaria's poems a similar interior dimension, although there is no "conversion," no Egypt or Promised Land. There is only the desert, that once was a river, a garden of Eden. St. Paul's spiritu-al journey was a linear trajectory; Annamaria's caravan is an attempted return, not to innocence, which is forever lost, but to the Eden of memory through a love renewed. Mortal lovers can hope for no more than that.

If the love celebrated in these poems is more real than the love of the *Song of Songs,* it is because the lovers themselves are more recognizably human. The poet's voice is vibrant and passionate. It can be nurturing ("the cloth that shields your mouth from the desert wind") or adversarial ("never reason with a woman/ she may think she has a brain"). Her friends will recognize in these shifting registers the sometimes mercurial passions that make her at once comforting and formidable. She can be submissive as Solomon's bride, but one recognizes in her submission a gathering storm. To sometimes mask her deepest sentiments, ostensibly to pass the time on caravan, she will tell stories, like a Scheherazade who is not the least intimidated by her Sultan. Some of the characters are vaguely reminiscent of the *Arabian Nights,* but they are tinged with unmistakable irony that will not always please her beloved. So much the worse for him, if he had been seeking the "dark but comely" love slave of biblical times.

Finally, the desert may be her theme, but the tenor of her voice is distinctly Mediterranean. Sails appear on the horizon, the tide laps at the shore, algae wash up on sand and the Sea salts her skin: traces of her native Italy abound in the arid landscape. Similarly, hints of her girlhood and first love, her filial piety and rebellion tempt the interpreter to read her lyrics as though they were narrative. She came to the North African desert as a traveler, but for the time she was there she brought more temperate sun and sea breezes to the parched land. The river is not hard to identify among the shifting sands. It is her refreshing poetic voice.

JOHN FRECCERO
New York University, New York

To Know
the Desert

Outsider

The maze opened
In a transparency of truth:
The travel begun so long ago
Coasted the shore
Defining contours, shapes.
You do not belong,
You are a stranger, she said

The maze opened,
Reading became unlimited
Understanding infinite
Separation underlined
Abstraction necessary
Living impossible.
You are a stranger, she said

Remote I go about my days
Rootless, loveless, selfless,
A city of the dead,
The reflection in the mirror says
Someone is there
The flesh, the bones, the shadow.
You are a stranger, she said

Detached I go about my days
Free not to be
Not to love
Not to give
Not to suffer
Do you know the price?
You are a stranger, she said

The stone I carry
— A weight in my pocket —
Is no passport:
Access is neither granted
Nor denied, I come and go
Traceless, invisible.
You are a stranger, she said.

The Day the Wisteria Dropped its Pods

They exploded
Small grenades,
Hitting the ground

I sat and listened
I startled and shivered
At each explosion

They fell
One by one:
They broke
They split
The seeds scattered
Black, polished, heavy,
Leaving the wrinkled
Desiccated skin

My life was measured
In each one of them —
I sat and listened:
In mockery
Blue jays echoed
The blasts,
Time fragments
Lay in between the stones

The desolate branches
Hung naked
Nowhere to hide their shame

Chimera

I will come
— She said —
To the waste land
Of your nights:

Make room,
Spread your thoughts
To my wings
As you would your body
To a lover,
Lift your head from the carcass
You feed on,
Breathe my breath,
Take my nipple into
Your mouth,
Take hold of my waist
And drink freely

I will color
Your dreams,
I will weave
Your memories,
I will drug
Your visions,
I will sing
Your rhymes

The red midnight sun
Points to the path between:
Mad shadows
Dance on the side,
Forests of willows
Bend to the center
The moon is about
To shed its shadow
Again,
Clouds suspend
Flowers on lance points
Of light

I will come
— She said—
To the waste land
Of your nights

Se Potessi Suonando
Richiamarti

Di musica sarebbero pieni i giorni
E le ore
E i momenti
In concerto immenso
Corale, epifanico
Di canti risuonerebbero
I giardini
E le strade
E gli spazi
In armonia perfetta
Universale, esultante

Ma il limite dell'umano
Delinea il possibile,
Circoscrive l'orizzonte,
L'incalzante muro della realtá
Nega la mano tesa a raggiungerti
L'occhio pronto a coglierti

Allora,
M'avvolgo di silenzio
E attendo

If, With Music, I Could
Evoke You

Of music would resound the days
And the hours
And each moment
In sweeping concert
Immense, epiphanic
Songs would fill
The gardens
And the streets
And the spaces
In perfect harmony
Universal, triumphant

Alas, the human limits
Outline the sterile want,
Circumscribe the horizon,
The unyielding wall of reality bars
The hand extended to touch you
The eye ready to surprise you

Then,
I lose myself in silence
And wait

Conoscere il Deserto

L'ho guardato
Con occhi arrossati, bruciati,
Mi sono rigirata nella sua sabbia
Granellata, infuocata,
Mi sono persa nei suoi venti
Delusi, inferociti,
Mi sono spenta nel suo sole
Abbagliato, sognato,
Aspettando l'eco

L'attesa non si é esaurita
Nello spazio d'un uomo
Ma la storia ha trovato la sua
        risposta:
Inutile, lungo ascolto,
La melodia creduta intravista
Spezzata
SILENZIO
— Feroce solitudine—
Permette saggezza infinita
Acrobazie d'incanto
Equilibri irreprensibili
Salite, discese accecanti
Senza rete:
La sabbia di sotto attende

To Know the Desert

I stared at it
With red, burning eyes,
I turned
In its grainy, fiery sand,
I lost myself
In its coarse, elusive winds,
I died
In its dreamy, glaring sun
Waiting for an echo

The measure of a life
Did not end the vigil
Yet history has found its answer:
Long, useless the listening,
The melody once glimpsed
Broken
SILENCE
— Savage solitude—
Grants unlimited wisdom
Dazzling acrobatics
Irreproachable balancing
Enchanting vaulting, blinding
        descent
Without a net:
Below the sand awaits

Requiem

Un anno ed un sogno fa

Il ricordo
Unico lascito:
Ombre i tuoi gesti,
Il tuo viso
Le tue mani
Pallenti
In un'incomprensibile lontananza

Hai lasciato
L'immenso peso
Della tua presenza
L'inenarrabile vuoto
Del tuo essere,
Realta'una nuova fase
Atrocemente irreale
                    Per sempre
Dolcissimo compagno perduto

Requiem

A year and a dream ago

Memory
Sole inheritance:
Shadows your gestures,
Your face
Your hands
Pale
In incomprehensible remoteness

You left
The immense burden
Of your presence
The unrelenting void
Of your being,
Reality a new phase
Atrociously unreal
                    Forever
Sweetest partner lost

Sorpresa

Trovarmelo
Nel cuore cosí
Quando credevo d'averlo perduto
Sentirmelo
Ancor vivo dentro
Mentre pensavo fosse morto

...E ricordare
I nostri inizi roventi
Quando sacerdoti di rituali nuovi
Spargevamo sangue
In sacrifici d'amore vietato,
Parole
Veicolo povero di linguaggio,
Pensieri
Spade guizzanti d'argento vivo,
Passioni, mitiche furie
Dove strumenti di due funzioni
Apprendevamo
Il significato d'un futuro
                impossibile

Surprise

To find it thus
In my heart
When I thought it lost
To feel it vibrate
Inside
When I thought it dead

...And remembering
Our flaming beginnings
When shamans of new rituals
We shed blood
In sacrifices of forbidden love,
Words
Imperfect means for our dreams,
Thoughts
Mercurial darting swords,
Passions, mythical furies,
Where instruments of two
                functions
We learned
The meaning of an impossible
                future

Rimpianto

Allora
Quando pallido, magro
Correvi sul filo d'una vita
Imprestata dal miracolo chimico
Vibravi
— Per contrasto —
In parole, gesti, slanci
Immensitá d'amore

S'alzava
Il sole con te
Si coricava,
La tua ombra riempiva i miei
          spazi,
Il futuro era sempre,
La notte
Lo squarcio luminoso contro
          cui
I nostri corpi disegnavano
Coreografie estenuanti

Nostalgia

At the time
When pale, thin
You ran on the edge of a life
Borrowed from the chemical
          miracle
You vibrated
— By contrast —
With words, gestures,
Bursts of infinite love

The sun rose
With you
And set,
Your shadow filled my space,
The future was forever,
The nights
Luminous openings against
          which
Our bodies designed
Exhausting choreographies

Lullaby

The heart is aching:
I bleed
Until it turns white,

Rock me tender

The heart is showing:
I lie
Until it is naked,

Cover me softly

The heart is crying:
I shout
Until it has no voice

Sing me a song

The heart is blushing:
I hide
Until it has no shame,

Sell me a slave

The heart is dying:
I live
Until it has no life,

Buy me a coffin

Italia Primo Amore

Vivere affiorati   sempre
In superficie
Bruciante, vissuta, intima, forte

Con l'alba della morte addosso   sempre
Col suono della vita dentro   sempre
Col profumo d'amore in fondo   sempre
Col mistero del fato intorno   sempre
Colla fatica di vivera accanto   sempre

Appartenere finalmente
Al sentimento familiare   sempre

Cedere ora al pianto collettivo

Soccombere oggi
Al sogno di domani giá perduto per   sempre

Italy First Love

To live on the surface   always
Burning, intense, intimate, strong

The dawn of death on   always
The sound of life within   always
The smell of love beneath   always
The mystery of fate around   always
The labor of life close   always

To belong finally
To the familial bond   always

To give in to the collective mourning

To surrender today
To the dream of tomorrow already lost   forever

To My Father

"Death will come
And will have your eyes"
And the wrath of time
And the longing of the past
And the menace of the present
And the thunder of the future

Will you dare to look?
On the mountain, with the prophet
Turn back only once
And see the evil
You cannot forget,
But remember only the good

Echoes pierce your heart
Break the walls
Fragment the air:
Hovering falcons are ready
To pluck your eyes

Choose well, my sweet,
The hollow nest of universality:
Weigh the stones
Balance the scale
Sift the sand
Collect the gold

Run thieving into the night

"Death will come
And will have your eyes."

(The quote is from Cesare Pavese)

Con Gente Mia

Ho detto, — ti ricordi —,
Di terra mia
Si chiude il cerchio,
L'alba d'un tempo chiarisce i cieli
Del remoto esotico distante nord

In te, con te
Riconosco memorie antiche:
— Odore di vino fresco
Bevuto con lo schianto del
                  bicchiere
Sul tavolo
— Sapore di baffi aspri
Passati con baci semplici
Sul viso
— Colore di voci roche
Parlate con toni forti
Nella sala
Della vecchia cantina
Che dava sul giardino

...E ancora:
Camino acceso
Fumo nei capelli
Cruogiolo nero
Polvere di ceneri calde
Bianchi tuberi arrosto
Grembiuli neri
Ciotole colme fumanti
Magia di trecce legate
Solenni racconti
Oscure paure di notte
Silenzi alti
A seguire lo spegnersi
Dell'ultima candela

Con forza
M'hai girata
M'hai indicato
La finestra sul cortile:
Sul davanzale
Un grande vaso a luci blu

With My People

— Remember, — I said,
Of my country
The circle is complete,
The dawn of old sweeps the
                          remote
Distant exotic northern skies

In you, with you
I live ancient memories:
— Smell of new wine
Drawn with the final slam
                  of the glass
On the table
— Flavor of pungent mustaches
Rubbed with simple kisses
On the face
— Color of hoarse voices
Spoken in loud tones
In the hall
Of the old cellar
Facing the garden

...And more:
Burning fireplace
Smoke in our hair
Black cauldron
Hot cinders' dust
White roasting tubers
Black aprons
Bowls filled with warm milk
Braids woven with magic
Solemn tales
Dark nocturnal fears
High silences
In the wake of the dying
Last candle

Forcefully,
You turned me around,
You pointed
To the window on the courtyard:
On the windowsill
A large vase with blue lights.

Per Lucia, per Livia

Tutto é venuto da lei,
Tu dici.
Fiamma nell'anima,
Ne parliamo,
Ride con noi.
Nessuno, hai detto,
Mi chiamerá piú,
Nessuno, hai detto,
Metterá la mano
Sulla mia spalla.
Rondoni disperati
Odo dal mio nido d'aquila
A cercarsi
Impazziti:
Paragono
L'alto, immenso grido
Del tuo silenzio
E ascolto.
La celebri come puoi
E lei diventa cascata rossa
Levigata pietra binaca
Riso felice
Caldo d'amore intenso
Da te venuto
In te, ora, sempre
Annunciatore di doni futuri:
Siedo alla tua soglia
E con gran pena
T'invidio

For Lucia, for Livia

Everything sprang from her,
You say.
A flame in your soul,
We speak of her,
She laughs with us.
No one, you said,
Will call me again,
No one, you said,
Will place a hand
On my shoulder.
From my eagle's nest
I hear desperate swifts
Madly searching
For each other:
I compare
The loud, immense sound
Of your silence
And listen.
You celebrate her as you can
And she becomes red waterfall
Polished white stone
Happy laughter
Warmth of intense love
Born of you,
In you now, forever
Messenger of future gifts:
I sit at your threshold,
In pain,
And look on, longingly

From the Karnak Poems

1. Karnak Night

Brown galabeia,
Gray turban fluttering in the dark
Descending,
Vaulting in sweeping motion
Squatting at each row
Offering again and again
Black liquid potions
In whispers,
One single glass left
Finally accepted.
The sound of time
Came to us
Across still sacred waters,
The lights of now
Evoked ancient deeds
Crimes we call history,
The weight of our nothingness
Distilled our thoughts
In pure cold silence:
Time stopped
In perfect suspended moments,
We belonged to the epic.　➡

2. Perhaps

You came with light
With sound
With night
You came,
You were unexpected
Three magic circles around the scarab
Saw the wish granted

You came across land
Across water
Across air
You came,
You were unforeseen
At dawn we parted with a promise
We kept by chance fulfilled

You came through desert
Through sand
Through field
You came,
You were untold
We said goodbye not knowing
What tomorrow would mean to a fable

And yet you came,
You were perhaps real

Dimenticarti.

Invento
Su corpi sconosciuti *le tue*
                    carezze,
Chiedo a bocche estranee
I fiori del *tuo* amore

Termino in orgasmi feroci
Le agonie infinite
Che avremmo potuto morire
                    insieme

Le dita, le mani,
La pelle di altri
Mi regalano echi d'amore
Che avrebbero potuto
                    apparten*erti*

To Forget You

On unknown bodies
I invent *your* caresses,
On unfamiliar lips
I pick the flowers of *your* love

I end in fierce orgasms
The infinite agonies
We could have died together

The fingers, the hands,
The skin of others
Grant me the echoes of love
That could have been *yours*

La Petite Mort You Give

White, blinding,
Delivering hidden memories
Without future:

Hardness made flesh
Aching, bleeding spur
Penetrates soft enclosures
You break the body
The mind follows
Pearls of pure pleasure flow
Probing
Possessive fingers convey
Burning sensations

In your eyes
Of Slavic stillness
The offering finds definite borders
In your violence, in your trespassing
Life, death
— Unimagined possibilities —
The womb a cave,
Hands of darkness
Hold the lightning shaft...
Tigellino, dispenser of freedom
Relieve my bondage

Cold Blue

Adamant refusals
Incite forbidden knowledge
Deadly game

Nordic teutonic
— Black man penis, nipples —
Shocking waves:

Cruel upmanship
Deviant pleasure sought, denied,
Dark fox
In pursuit of past flesh
Half seen, unknown, foreboding
— Ancient medicine, needles,
Ecstasy of abandonment,
Weightless,
Images fast, below, beyond:
Mountain spurs
Glacial beauties blue
Never ending
Eyes changing
Shapes fast, fast —

Your mind
Without light
Forest of wonder

Mensch

Sensations, depths denied.
Abstention.
Eyes to parry
To reveal restrained balance
Seemingly perfect

Yours
Object to surrender
For how long?
Sands of time will know:
Paths, infinite signs,
The rushing of stars precipitate
The chemical upheaval
So easy to hurt, to maim, to wane
Desert landscape
Flutter beyond relentless horizons
— Apocalypse now —
No knights
Only headless horsemen to madness apt

Do Not Judge Those Children

The anger
Transparent in the fear
Of those tormented eyes

The love
Burning in the souls
Of those ravaging fathers, mothers

Strangling
Drowning
Dragging those children
Through dusty roads of failed love

Those children
They say they love
Those children
They sweep away
From one cradle to another,
Pawns on a chess board,
Prisoners of other people's games,

Those children
Whose destiny is bargained,
Bought and sold
— Merchandise at a flea market —
Those children
Rich fountains
Drained by premature despair

Those children
Miracles of high wire balancing,
Those children who learn
Defeated how to conquer...

Do not judge those children

Again

Green blue waters
Mesmerize the eyes
Define the frontiers of desire
Paralyze the will
And liquid magnets
Pull the laboring soul
In a horizon of no return

Again

Tender, tender is the touch:
The flesh pierced
The heart violated
The mind erased,
Reflections point the way
Break the future in a thousand fragments
With the noise of a whisper

Again

Hands, faces
Compose the magic circle
Confine the thoughts to now:
We stand on the edge together

Again

Understanding: October 17, 1989

Nothing would change…
If you died, no one would mourn.
An ancient witch,
You accept your fate
Prescribed, inscribed
Foreseen, unavoidable,
An alchemist, you live your experiments,
The potion is yours to drink.
The risk of arriving late at a party
Is that the games have been played,
Everything already said and done:
You are always late, you seem to be.
Exclusion translates into uniqueness, aloofness,
Violator of sacred thresholds you turn to ashes

Can you divine the distant writing?
An unusual temple,
An unsuspected ritual
Requiring neither offers, nor sacrifices
Nor incense burning,
The high priestess grants all
But does not extend her hand
For reciprocation,
Her knowledge has sealed her
In a transparent chamber
She can never leave:
Enter, listen to the music,
Play, pray
Then say goodbye

(October 17, 1989 was the date of the Loma Prieta earthquake)

The Snake Charmer

You spoke
You read
You sang
Your music played on
Aware of your power
You watched our coils
Fold into submission:

Gone the anger
Forgotten the toil of living
We quivered in wait...
Your name

     Victory flag
Your face

     Furrow of a thousand winds
Your eyes

     Receptacle of many reflections
Your hands

     Shaman's instruments

You officiated the ceremony
You sounded the future
You celebrated life

Welcome

High on your pedestal
You thought yourself safe, you
                              hid:

See no love
Hear no love
Do no love
Feel no pain,
A child's play your creed
"You love pain"
A year ago you said,
Mistaking my agony
For pleasure,
And you continued
To burrow deeper,
Your tools
Silver and crystal
Pewter and jade
Diamonds and rubies
Silk and brocades
"Can you forget your soul,"
                              I asked
"Not now, not now" you said
You went about
Your beauty perfect
Your eyes shut

Unreachable goddess
Untouched . . .
Then the Indian summer
Laid a gift
At your feet:
It touched your heart
It opened your soul
Sister now more than ever,
Welcome to the human
                              condition!
No 21 gun salute
No celebration, no flags
No firecrackers, no cheers
Simply *"yes, it was time"*
Will mark
Your intimation of mortality:
Brave amazon,
Wear your armor,
Ride your winged horse,
Unsheathe your sword,
Fight the agonies of your mind
The burden of living,
Come to the edge

Eating

To be
Equated to food:
I am eaten, devoured
Hardly tasted
Digested, forgotten

On to another dish

Who am I
I ask
You say my name, why?
I satisfy your appetites:
Entrées do not have feelings

Desire and Separation: A Triad

1. Transfixed

She lay once more
Slave
Pinned to the pillow by his stare,
His commands, his will

Tides of past ebbed in,
New blue waters
Drowned residues
Of shipwrecked rebellion

Hot cinders blew past the shore
Surprised the mountain
Split the marble fountain

In the plain, the caravan slept well that night
Dreaming of unknown seas
Softly rocking crystal pebbles

2. Quando

Il seno
Memore di maternitá non vissuta
Offro alla tua bocca
Alle tue manni

Quando

Il grembo
Come corolla accesa di maggio
Apro al tuo sguardo
Ai tuoi baci

Allora
Mi sorprende il pianto:
Il sofferto non é la violenza
Il torto antico, il tuo trionfo...
L'eco della solitudine sovrana
Annega ogni altro senso
Cancella ogni possibilitá d'intesa
Respinge le sponde
Apre l'abisso di separazione

I detriti dell'amore consumato
Sola testimonianza d'un
                    tentativo
Di comunicare

Imperativo
É ricominciare

2. When

My breasts
Barren to motherhood
I give to your mouth
To your hands

When

My womb corolla burning
With May fever
I open to your eyes
To your kisses

Then
Unexpected tears well up:
Suffering is not for the violence
The wrong of old, the male
                    triumph...
Solitude echoes sovereign
Drowns any other sense
Annuls any possibility of
                    understanding
Widens the banks
Exposes the abyss of separation

The debris of spent love
Sole witness of an attempt
To communicate

It is imperative
To begin again

3. Voglio

La *mia* notte
A viverla con te
Nei nostri silenziosi lunghi
Disperati abbracci
Ciascuno
Chiuso nelle sue trame antiche
Di tradimento, di dubbio...

Ho smesso d'affilare i coltelli
Spegni tu i fuochi di guerra
Celebra la luce con me
Lascia
Che venga l'alba a spezzare
I gradi di separazione

3. I want

My night
To live it with you
In our silent, long
Desperate embraces
Both locked
In ancient webs of betrayal
And doubt...

I have stopped sharpening my
                              knives
You could douse your war fires
And celebrate the light with me
Let
The dawn break
The degrees of separation

Awakening

1. Death

Roaring
At the shores of consciousness
It asked admittance.
Time bled in segments
Of staccato blue
And crescendo yellow:
Fiery tongues licked the wounds
Inhaling life, consuming.
The unjust marvel of it
Brought revelation
Shattered the fortress
Broke down the forest
Invited darkness

2. Acceptance

It came with the promise of thunder,
With the dark mystery of innocence.
Smooth, impassible highways
Snaked through the mountains
Consigning magenta hues
To white scattered dwellings
Suited to children's ancestral memories.
There, at the intersection,
The womb split and received
The reluctant exile.
Light flung open the window
Darkened the shadows
Stretched corners into linear succession of walls.

3. Repast

We feasted at the dawn of future.
We were made of stone. Untouchable.
Compelled to devour, we tasted life,
Pausing at the source.
Shadows grew out of our eyes
And cast spells in a circle
Blinding the night into submission.
Slaves, we conquered our bondage,
We reigned in our masters,
Lawless, we searched the Plain
Never looking back
At the corpses on the road:
"Power is mine" sayeth our creed.

We collected wild mushrooms
That bloomed in the summer.

Of Deserts and Rivers

Caravans

The desert at Sakkara, Egypt.

When the Desert Was a River...

Caravans
Led by blue men
Stop at the well:
They drink, they trade, they rest...
Quivering, coarse palaces,
Stretch against the dreamy vapors

The fortuneteller sits in the shade,
Darting black slits watch mutely...
She knows, leaves in a cup told her
She dreams of the scent of white magnolias,

Jacarandas swirl their blue radiance
— A menace to oblivion —
Work the magic of the thread
Embroider the virgin linen

She hums rhymes and juggles stones
She soars in slow, silent circles
Above tired flesh
Consumed consuming consummated
She senses the water, she smells it,
Her probable sons used to bathe in it

When the desert was a river...
Carved silver rang to summon
Raging islands of thoughts fresh from the source...

The fortuneteller sits in the shade,
She hums rhymes and juggles stones

In the Maghreb, Morroco.

The stories of a thousand and one days are in the form of poems to be read at breakfast, at bedtime, and at all the other times of our lives.

Sitting with a Loved One Across a Table in the Early Morning is Cruel

Wrinkles show at their best
Frowns are most virulent,
Yet one starts as always,
Continues the debates, the words of yesterday
Uhm!! Cute hat,
You said,
So I wore it in ludicrous combination
With my short silk gown,
But the day began with a smile
And we had breakfast in semi-victorian fashion.
You read the paper:
Temperatures are rising,
The stock market is down, oh! God!
About the murdered girl, poor angel,
We chatted on
Old friends exchanging views most comfortably

We agreed we were in consonant accord
So I told you a fable,
One from the stories of a thousand and one days.

Lovers' Rhyme

To him she said
You are my country

He did not reply

To him she said
You are my border

He did not reply

To him she said
You are my source

He did not reply

To him she said
You are my present

He did not reply

To him she said
You are my mind

He replied thank you
Went to the market
Bought invisible ropes
Tied her down
Readied a coffin

She sat in it and said
I'll wait and then I'll die

To which came his

Swift Reply

I came upon a river
Flowers on each bank
Rustling noise in high trees
Forest perfect
Perfume and wind conjured visions
I longed to make mine
I waited
Then night fell
And covered my heart

My turn, she said and she told the story of

The Drunken Maid

She was eighteen
Chaste and beautiful, she wore white

She met a Knight
Noble and strong
He wore silver and blue

He sang to her
He jousted for her
He killed for her

She cooked for him
She slaved for him
She lied for him   ➡

Together
They drank to life
Oh, they drank,
They feared no one

They walked on air
On wind,
On high wires

He fell one day and she with him
From air, from grace...

He left her a legacy
His heart,
His love and his wine

He paused and then

How Long

Can love last, he asked
She said don't ask

But I must, he replied
I have lost so many times
A gambler with lead dice
A tinker with broken pots
A king with no kingdom
Naked the halls of my palace

No more
No more,
She said,
I can give you visions
I can play for you
I can color your dreams
I can,
I will...

The City of Gold, the Kasbah Road, Morocco.

He did not acknowledge it and told her the story of

The Forbidden City

It sprang from the desert
Houses of gold
Sky of indigo blue
Its beauty a legend...

I came to it with my lover
The city welcomed us in its splendor
Silk and damask brushed our skins
Jasmine and magnolia scents drugged our thoughts
Purple and violet hues touched our hearts
Music and rhymes played in our hair

I trembled and asked her to pledge
Never to say I love you

She agreed not knowing how cruel it would be
How hard...

I pained with her and yet
The rules were set
The game was played

One night,
When the iridescence of colors
The music and the perfumes and the air
Reached the suspended perfection of dreams
She cried out my name and broke her oath

The city vanished and I turned to stone

She said she had heard the thoughts of

The Forsaken Bride

And when you leave
Your eyes still on my mind
Your smile still in my gaze
Your smell still in my womb
Your hands still on my skin
Your hair still in my fingers,
The arduous nocturnal journey begins.

Your dark mystery
Guards the secret
The distance,
Kindles the anxiety
The tension
Changes time in my enemy
Dawn in my executioner
Makes me a prisoner

The Great Mosque, Casablanca, Morocco.

He sighed and spoke of

The Desert Rider

No longer I wait by the white window sill
No longer sit in the gray courtyard
No longer bathe in the blue fountain

A black caftan my home
A dark horse my destiny

I ride to my beckoning future
Away from my uncertain yesterday

I can stay only a while

I can smell only one rose

I can sing only one song

Moroccan Riders, Marrakesh, Morocco.

Have you heard the lament of the faithful wife? she asked

Where Am I

In your life
Am I the dawn or the sunset
Am I the middle of the day or dusk
Am I a button in your shirt
The lace in your shoe
The water for your camel
The canvas of your tent
Or the cloth that shields your mouth from the desert wind?

Am I the fresh cold drop of the night
That lingers on your dry forehead
Melting,
Sweeping away
The dark thoughts wrought by the exhausting journey

Where am I in your life

Whisper it, but say it

Do you know what the old philosopher said?
And he told her

Never

Be gentle to a woman
She may think you are weak

Never reason with a woman
She may think she has a brain

Never show admiration
She may think she has your heart

Never buy her one slave
She may want 25

Never give her signs of love
She will want all of you

Be kind to yourself
And demand of her
To be...
More like a man

Murmurs to the Desert Wind
(How can I tell the many wonders...)

At night, my arms around me, I quietly recoil,
Confide to my skin what I failed to say before.
Quietly, I whisper to myself I love you,
Ever so quietly in the dark hours, ever so quietly...

                    Do you know my love,
The many wonders of you: your
Eyes, a gateway to your emotions,
Hands pressing on my side,
Weight crushing the smallness of me,
Breath blowing softly against my hair,
Skin surging under my palms,

                    Do you know my love,

The briefest moment becomes the longest
Only to disappear in a cigarette's lifespan.
Time, the enemy, running through days
With merciless sword, slashing past and present,
Stirs old and recent coals and ashes...

                    Do you know my love,   ➡

The many wonders of you:
Your light step crossing the threshold,
Your studious look when reading
Your voice humming ancient rhymes
The uncountable sparkles of your smile
The luminous brilliance of your hair

Quietly, I whisper, ever so quietly,
In the dark hours of the night
                    Do you know my love,
The many wonders of you…

Lioness

Her prey
In silk ribbons and strands of leather
She holds

Her willing victim
From her rich wet lips
Receives sweet death

She asks she takes she gives
Her glory
In rituals of power

Her eyes tell stories
Of depths explored,
Primeval secrets

She knows
Fascination domination
Destruction resurrection

She promises pain and delivers pleasure

Persimmon

His mouth closed on the orange globe
As if it had been a woman's breast.
The bite severed half the fruit
Lingered on the red moist flesh...

The soft sweet pulp invaded his tongue,
Motioned the giant wave forward:
He ate into his inglorious childhood,
Wonders of another time—
Blinding white memories—
Rushed in

He savored the unknown beauty to come from his seed

Tangiers, Morocco.

Solitude So Perfect

That a noisy crowd
Does not disrupt

That a deserted mall
Wooes and completes

That a concerted sound
Underlines and polishes

That a droning discourse
Does not disturb

Laughter intersects
The linear structure
Falling in perpendicular

The emperor's clothes
Are so befitting
Nakedness hides everything

The author at 40.

At 40

I think, I listen, I wait...
I explain, I surrender, I go forward
I suffer, I sing, I dream

I grow in passion
I withdraw cold

I rise in happiness
I fall in rage

Erratic: lost in thought, alert, dreaming, loving,
Repenting, angry, suffering, delirious, lonely
Brilliant, colorless, all at once

How difficult to know oneself

Untitled

SILENT   IMMENSE   DESERT

Solitude

Is

The Small Pyramids at Giza, Egypt.

Morning in Monument Valley

Exploding, crushing primeval light,
White dawns, blinding
Red red red sand, ancient,
Soft furrows, red red red faces

Time stands still in the valley,
Wind blows rocks to dust
Under a distant god's blessing
Immutable, unmoving, unforgiving

Genesis

—This is my realm —
He embraced the red sand
—This is my bed—
He held the salty waters
—This is my house—
He sat on the naked mountain

He shook his staff and dropped a seed
Giants moved the sky, planets trembled:
His laughter echoed loud through infinite space

More

The 2000 year old parable
Speaks of solitude:
He too, in the garden,
Betrayal all around him,
Sometimes thrice repeated,
Stood, alone, to bear the trial,

                      Alone

Son of Man, Son of God,
When, in the shadows of Gethsemane,
The call came
Sweet smells around you,
Still grace, silver leaves above,
You held fast to Your faith,
For all to witness

                      Alone

The injurious curses, the tortured flesh
Misunderstood, belittled, debased.
It was impossible
For the tender Mother to collect your tears,
Son of Man, Son of God, You stood
Alone, to bear the trial,

                      Alone

Your only fault
The fervor of innocence,
Your only shield
Your belief
You dreamt of rescuing mankind,
A scapegoat, you met cruelty,
Trapped in treachery
You stood, alone, to bear the trial

                      Alone

Time

The author at 16.

The Passage of Time or
The Limbo of the Mediterranean

In this land which is no longer mine,
In this land that I wear like a shirt,
In this land which weighs upon me
With its ancient cargo of memories and death,
I feel divided, ripped apart, undone

I stretch out, as ever,
In this sea, immersed, with
The horizon blurred at the line
Where water and land merge,
And there the passage of boats,
In flight from the binding shore,
Marked by white trails.

As reflected in a mirror,
I see one which, having
Slipped its moorings,
Pushes its stern aimlessly forward

I stretch out as ever
In this sea, immersed
Divided, ripped asunder
Between past and present,
Doing and being, living and dying.

It is in this way
That I devour
My wait in limbo

Harvest House

This spring rolled in with hurried speed,
—And the acquiescence of death.

It broke the stream with a thousand scintillating visions,
Gave the measure of the season's ending game
We no longer visit the marketplace,
We play solitaire, now, in front of a mute screen,
We escalate in a terminal direction.

Then, when the harvest was ripe
We locked the gates.
Then, when the harvest was rich,
We sang the night.
Then, when the harvest was ours,
We dreamt the morning.

The skin was alabaster,
Maggots nested elsewhere
And plucked unknown fields.

The house was pure,
Dolphins rested on the walls
And carried boys on their backs

Then, when the harvest was ripe...

The Great Market Khan-el-Khalili, Cairo, Egypt.

Once Again

Ours the night, the ocean, the lights
Giants from another time
We invented the future,
For ever suspended in our web

Loneliness, despair seemed
Defeated, vanquished.
The dream was alive while

We wove the threads of a tenuous canvas

Policastro, September 1994

At peace, away, far,
Anxiety forgotten
And violence with it.
Long, sweeping birds
Accenting the horizon in close flight

The noise of man comes distant
Stays on the threshold, without invading

Time no longer a measure.
Nobody knocks, not even memory.

The author at age 7, Naples, Italy.

Paths

Take me as I am now, — she says, I am tired, the tide
is high and the shore is receding: it is hard to wash
the ruined clothes and to fill the empty cupboard.
Doors slam in the distance against used feelings and
hasten the fall.

1.

It was no time to be a child: Her tutelage was of a
different nature: fear stilled her play and hungry mouths
devoured her age. The odd year 7 saw her innocence
bloom in shame and pointed the way to things to come,
legends roamed the sky, yet she walked in sand,
she wore ribbons in her hair and braided her heart.

Take me as I am now, — she says, I am the eyes of the
children of others, their hearts, their tears, their
wrongs...I have lived forever, I bear the markings...
my sister, the hyena, feasted with me the other night:
we moved slowly in the high grass, we ate well...
close drums chased us away.   ➡

2.

And I love them all, — she says, open books of resigned
tolerance — the index too long to be of importance —
the pages innumerable: the silent child drifting in the
dark, the painted woman clutching a dream, the lonely
man expiating the past. Their agony in the sentence
pronounced long ago: how could the weights be so
unbalanced, the cards so uneven?

Where is the just design, the fair retribution? Blind
executioners swing the pendulum hold the prisoners
in wait for the amorous strike of deliverance.

3.

And I love them all, — she says, I want to hold them
all, I want to to soothe their wounds, I want to brush
their hair, I want to invent their future...open the
gates, sell the horses, the jewels, the slaves and pay
the ransom of pain.

The arches of the Imperial Stables in Meknes, Morocco.

Small Abstract Things

Arabesque

Tonight of all nights, I dig in the well of memory
I walked on smooth pebbles, on rough cliffs,
On jagged edges, on sand I walked,
I tiptoed, I burrowed, I skipped,
I jumped, an acrobat in flight.

1. The Poetry Man

You rode the night, suddenly an actor,
With eyes of fire, you spoke, your tongue aflame
Against webs of luminous darkness, of Lorca, of gypsy love,
Of Granada exploding like a watermelon,
A pendulum between real longings and disturbing harmonies.
Your folly — by few understood — translated
In an unacceptable tender, violent offer.

2. The Champagne Man

You, adrenaline flaring, a child,
Transformed, happy, a pleasure to the mind,
Pursued — a gymnast — dazzling paths of thoughts.
You charmed the stunned listener
With melodies soothing to a cobra.
You enraveled the dark tangles of my soul,
You gave me newfound innocence   ➡

3. The Sense of Time

The present, pressing, penetrating,
Disrupts convolutions of future memories,
The past, rielaborating constant cosmic circuits
Consumes spirals of present coals and ashes.

Memory, a febrile cycle of revolving doors,
Carries suspended discourses, bound in honest contrast.

Fluid words touch unknown margins, banks,
Searching for a common secret existence

Late — immensely late, the stars,
The planets of another time appeared tonight.

Early — immensesly early, pollution, corruption
Ushered in the space of another life

From an eagles' nest I spy the water:

Salt, on the distant shore, is gaining ground.

Flowers on the door of a Moroccan house.

And When It's Time

All in my unkindness will be
With two unerring judges presiding.

On red and chrome stools
Angels perch at the bar
I marvel at the order of the company,
They ignore the writing on the mirror
And ask for another beer.

He asked if we knew the message,
We questioned in return HIS existence
We ignited his fire.
Prometheus is unbound, I said,
Unclean and vengeful,
No time for heroes, I said,
He spoke of a dream, a mission,
He was off, to New Hampshire, he said.

John Milton's
*Leviathan has lost,

Now no time for heroes

Now no cause for rebellion.

*John Milton, *Paradise Lost*, Book 1

It Feels Like Friday Today

Time drops the hours
Measured one by one
Into the glass case
Slowly...
Silence fills this vacuum we call life,

I learn the meaning of oblivion
And pass by open windows, tempted.

The cards on the table
Reveal complicated paradigms
Of casual importance

I play solitaire and long for Monday
A very normal day
                When I exist again

White

Clutched to the last
Island of ice where the North
Begins its downward slide,
The brilliance of it all spreading
Not gradual, not gently,
Rather with violent, all arresting totality.

Stillness, silence,
Solitude so perfect.

Cold, calm, glacial.

White on white, footprints
Ending nowhere, indicate
Attempts of desperate flights.
An Arctic fox, white on white,
Starves on the immense blinding expanse
And longs for the comfort of the impending night.

Comet

(for Marilyn)

Primordial, luminous, soft, eternal you were.
Woman, part of me, of all of us before we came to the
                  mortification
Of equality, symbol of oneiric feminine remembrances
You stood so close, accessible, open, innocent
And always misunderstood

Blatant abuse drove the sword that ended your life.
Sister to all women you knew the beginning of time,
The end of time — but would not break
You would not disappear, bleeding, hurt
Your soul of a thousand mirrors
With no reflections of love
Still sends your image to us
Across the dark of space.

Reflection: Not Liking Tapestries

They hang straight, I am crooked
They are defined, I, confused
They are precise, I, nebulous
They are noble, I am not
They are stable, I, unpredictable

Perfect images smile coldly
Frozen in ancient memories:
Birds caught in still flight
Lifeless dogs stand sadly aside
Joyless children sit and stare

I do not relate to tapestries

Rich churchmen strut about
Princes ride their fat horses
Bedecked in royal attire,
Unknown destinations waiting
They make a pretty, pretty scene

Venerable saints pour blood
From gushing wounds while
Performing impossible miracles,
Raise the dead, heal the sick.
The populace applauds, unmoved.

I do not relate to tapestries

They are immortal, I am mortal
They are cold, I, fire
They speak of perfection, I, incomplete,
They are silent, I am noise
They are fantasy, I am flesh

Doubtless, I do not like tapestries

Song

I heard his voice the other night
Many sounds mixed in it
Whisper, thunder, music
Rolling on the high dunes

I no longer hope
I no longer dream

Creatures no longer sing to me
From cliffs in crushing straits
Rhymes no longer come to me
Blazing through the air

I no longer hope
I no longer dream

Lead me through empty halls
Lead me through dark corridors
Where I can rest my eyes
Lost in darkness without end

I no longer hope
I no longer dream

The Sybil's Invitation

Come in, she whispered, tea is served,
Come in, Tiresias is waiting;
The garden breathes sweet scents,
Pink peonies open their purses
And fade quickly into the short night.

Come in, she whispered, tea is served,
The pomegranates are cut, the figs are sweet,
We can play cards later, the three of us.

Under the camphor tree we will braid tales
And cast spells, mortals will come and listen,
Will wonder, will know not our weakness.

Flaming tripods smoke my chambers,
Terrible echoes travel through narrow passages,
Frighten the visitors into believing an old woman's words.

Our glory is no more, Pythia,
Yet we were the womb of the world.
A storm brews in the north,
It must be yours, Tiresias, it has the signs:
Let the clouds assemble,the thunder break,
Let the rain come and still our thoughts.

Come, let us drink to who we were,
The pomegranates are cut, the figs are sweet.

A storm over Bryce Canyon, Utah, USA.

Quietly, Into the Night

We go back in time
When the future was still to come
And death knocked at other doors.

Children of the moment, we celebrated.

We drank, we dreamt.
Absence was not yet possible.

Solemn in our beliefs, we wrote our stories
With the devotion of novices and the rage of youth.

As in a train, visions of past landscapes
Appear fleetingly in the window frame:
We stare longingly and dream of
New solutions for an old world

The poet at age 3 with her beloved governess Maria, and her brother Mario, at a fascist parade in Naples, Italy.

Today I Smelled the Sea

You did too, you said...
Will you walk back with me
To the far shore where — without memory —
I used to play?

Then, in resplendent solitude,
I rode a wooden horse into the horizon
Raced the elusive brothers below the keel.

I was the sun child: hair turned gold,
Salt on the skin gave wings to flight
The sky was close and the stars were mine.

I counted them one by one,
At dawn, I stole the brightest
And wore it on my chest.

Mother questioned the gift,
I lied and said "God's"

The island of Procida, Naples, Italy.

The White of the Wolf

They walked softly through their hearts' darkness,
Talked of things past and of those yet to come,
Their breaths drew disconcerting designs in
The air thick with the smell of burned wood,
Their bones white with fear of unacceptable loss.

I wonder if this is life...she whispered.

Giant fires blazed here and there
Set the mountain alight.

The cold, cold night was only a dream.
Solitary grey wolves lay curled
Silent in snowy meadows,
Their half-opened eyes waited
For the next shadow to cross the moon
Their skins mortal, their vision divine.

I wonder if this is life...she whispered

Spring

April promises
A spring of agonies,
A cruel string
Of unsung melodies,
A ritual
Of unknown flesh

Your face carves threats into my future.

Fog

Liquid wet banks
Undiscovered splendor overflows in the dark
Nocturnal magic of tenderness
Lived, imagined, dreamt, lost,
Halts pain in time-suspended
Perfect moments.

Signs

Lights conjure magic in the garden tonight:
Puck is everywhere, sauntering about.
And I remember
Another garden in Georgia, by the cemetery.

A hundred fireflies lit the ground,
Gave respite to the black of the grass
High around the ankles,
I held hands with the giant from the North
And believed the fable I was living.

The peach colored jacket shone against the darkness,
And I felt like a fruit, round, soft, happy.

We stood silent,
New stones against old ones
By the cemetery.

Our faces wet, perhaps by tears, perhaps not,
We trembled at the shape of the moment

Fear held our hearts, we knew
Tomorrow had yet to come

Traces

Do not wither, do not fade
By the merciless toils of living consumed,
I could not bear to witness
The unpleasant passage of time on you!

The smell of your body in mine,
The soft curve of your hips in my eyes,
The mark of your weight on my breasts,
The calm breath of your mouth on my face

Thus, forever, I say, I will guard your memory
As I go forward on the path leading me away
From you into earth's dark womb, the one
That foreshadows the terrifying loss of you.

Perhaps, just perhaps, nostalgia of me
Will surface in you too, perhaps, on others
You will consume the memory of my skin
That once granted you sublime oblivion.

Love &
Beyond

Cartwheeling

The moon is heavy,
Large, red, and full of mist.

Blood trails in the sky turn grey
At the tip of the crescent,
They drip distilled dew
Into the lonely mariner's heart
Fighting to keep alive
While sailing
On the raging waters below.

I sit, gaze, in silent wonder
At the many lives I have lived,
At the many lives I witnessed.

Surrender, the light whispers,
Resist, whisper the shadows

In the Midnight Garden of Good and Evil
I walk the thin line, trying to stay balanced
And ask to be forgiven in a loud voice.

Islander

Rocks bloom in the uncertainty of dawn
And long for the warmth
                        Of noon.
A thousand stars fell last night
Burned the water with the sizzling noise of hot steel.

Flesh lay exposed for all to see
And walls of thoughts rose in mourning tides.

Searching eyes roam the listless horizon
And long for the whiteness of
                        A sail.

Vision

Arrogant
Unmoved by my wound,
Persecutor, herald
Flame the sword,
Ice the wings —
You distilled vials
Of unannounced death.

You ushered in
An atrocious unforeseen future,
Faraway thresholds.

Cocoon

And when the door closes
The tryst begins.

We are, you and I,
Secret accomplices
In the crime of love,

The magic box unfolds its treasures,
One by one.

We rejoice playfully, solemn at times,
Symphony celebrating togetherness.

We read, we reason, we love, we dream.
Intense, oblivious, happy
We are You and I.

The Would-be Collector

And I am left behind...

He leaves more free
Than when he walked in.

His stride firm, proud,
Breaks invisible waves.

I weigh a little more, instead,
Anchored down by fresh
Thoughts of nocturnal intimacy.

I live again
The magic of gestures,
Tender correspondence.

And I want more of this
Fleeting communion.

Definition insists
From inside to become
The reality of existence.

If I could pin all
The butterflies down
In a large, rich display!

However, they would be dead.

Smell

As I lie in bed — our bed now —
The smell of you — the night smell —
The subtle vapor of your skin rises around,
About, above me.

As I lie in bed — our bed now —
The other side of midnight — the morning side
Rolls into brief numbers and hastens dawn.

As I lie in bed — our bed now —
My white white breasts,
Pointed globes of waiting flesh
Rise softly in full view.
Longing for the touch of a hand — be it gentle or cruel.

As I lie in bed — our bed now —
Your face drops in the calm of sleep,
Dark well of oblivion,
Stretches its lines in smooth marks of no importance,
Offers no resistance to the amorous inspection.

As I lie in bed — our bed now —
Your strong strong arms behind your head,
Become fluid forms of power.
They forget the bodies they encircled, the hands they held,
Leave me wondering
Whom they are embracing now

As I lie in bed — our bed now —
The smell of you — the night smell —
Moors me to your side like a ship at the dock.

Surprise Factor

Melodies in cruel sequence
Crowd the mind
Unexpected, unsought, unwanted
The weight crushes
Thoughts once in wantoness become free.

Burnt ashes the desires of before:
One sharp, icy pain
Punctuates my days,
The promised date
Incites me on through yet another hour,
Notes from the mechanical box
Soothe the anxious wait.

We, Righteous Men and Women

When we lie awake in the early morning,
They come and lay siege,
They come to stay.
Some disguised,
Some in the crude light of reason,
New Mongols to the restless mind,
Warriors of life, they bring the gift of understanding.

How can we, righteous men and women, sleep
And not heal the disharmony
In this conspiracy of ours? Look back then,
Not in anger, but in love,
Try to explain the *natural order:*

The friend who died last year, the one
No one could either heal or save,
The Father she knew so little,
Whose wisdom she knew too late,
The husband who raised her
Whom she will for forever mourn,
The girl who said "I love you" not meaning it,
The man who yesterday, for the first time,
Called out her name and healed her heart,
The frightened child, one more victim of ancient hatred,
Dying by violent hands on the West Bank,
The rebels in a faraway land
Who fall to prevent the taking of one more oil field... ➡

We acquiesce, in the name of *natural order,* we acquiesce
And with RANDOM ACTS OF KINDNESS
We appease the disturbed conscience.

Let us don the red hoods of shame and
Mend this chorality of pain, let us
Cast stones in the mirror and
Rise in a flame of indignation.

Let us shake these indifferent shells and
Feel the nails in our beds.

How can we, righteous men and women,
Side with Hamlet and "perchance dream"?

Rage

From covenant to covenant,
Diagonal travel
Intersects points of light.

Caught, we circle the narrow space
With eyes of flame
And rarely rest in quiet corners.

The raised arm reveals the rage
Which ate the flesh of the bone
And exposed the ruptured tendons.

Caught, we gaze at the opening
With hearts of lead
And long for the searing pain of living.

— Begin again — he says,
But the corners are filled with shadows
And the mute dialogue turns into a
Deafening empty monologue.

— Talk to the dead — he says,
But the starving child is always there
Crowned sovereign of all actions
He cannot speak to anyone.

— Let go — he says,
But distance bleeds the heart white
Killing the flowers born of the crimson tree
That not long ago promised a good harvest.

How to mend
The buried wrongs, the unspoken words
That cut into the flesh in feverish toil
Directions are incorrect,
They lead nowhere.
Dimensions of desert landscape occupy the vision,
Roll the days into moving dunes, frantic vortices,
Forever changing, forever still.

Messengers of anger, we
No longer rest in the yellow softness,
No longer swim in the transparent blue.

The quick sand, the murky turbulence
Still stir ancient guilts, instigate new rage,
Call the living to the dead.

Separation one step away,
One sole act of will of casual importance
Will breed blind, deaf, mute children
Without faces, without tomorrows.

Pietro, the poet's beloved husband.

Requiem II

"Let us go, let us go then," You and I and the shadows
Wading through canals, at night
Remembering the times, remembering the words
Too many spoken quietly with tears ready to fall,
Too many spoken harshly with anger mounting

"Let us go, let us go then," You and I and the shadows.
We climbed together, we walked, we ran together
Soaring high, we had a life to invent,
And one to remember.
It was like going through corridors,
Pictures lining the sides, openings into another time,
Voices whispering: we held hands and each other.

"Let us go, let us go then," You and I and the shadows
Our only defense love,
Love invented, love imagined, perhaps real,
They said it would not last,
It could not: defiant, we went into exile,
Hiding was dangerous, it made us stronger

I hold a ghost in my hands now
Shapeless, eyes dug out, hollow,
A smile appears only to fade, quickly,
Into the last image of death.

"Let us go, let us go then," You and I and the shadows.
We still play bridge, you and I, silent partners
While the winner bids grand slams,
You and I, we still play bridge and hedge the bet   ➡

I am not a gambler, remember, you were,
You played so well, so daring,
I just went along, by chance, docile.

We still play bridge, you and I, silent partners
We bid against dark prophecies of death and ruin.
Then we laughed and went on to paint the sky,
We won the bet, again and again.

We did not look back and I surrendered,
The blind augur whispered to the wind,
Thunder broke his spell, swept the plane
We did not know defeat.

How can I tell what went on? Between us?
Locked in our world, we said little
The Cabal worked and we drew magic circles
On the walls of our souls.

"Let us go, let us go then," You and I and the shadows
Wading through canals, at night.

"Let us go, let us go then," from T.S. Eliot's
The Love Song of John Alfred Prufrock

Juggler

The curtain up,
He balances his lance.
Free, happy, mercurial,
A delight to the viewer,
He makes loops and sticks swirl, weightless:
His ability, magical
At every turn, produces the winning ace.

Breathless,
Spectators watch the ancient plot unfolding
Dazzled, powerless, ensnared...
The final bow comes suddenly,
Applause is not required.
The end, like the beginning,
Is quick, mysterious, innocent.

Rita and Antonio, the poet's parents, 1927, Sorrento, Italy.

Years Later

Mother is no longer,
Suddenly adulthood, a reality,
Nowhere home, nowhere safety.

Loneliness around, inside,
Churning in endless twists.
Sterile existences hang
From nameless tree
Truncated, cut off.

Clouds, suspended, smile briefly
Only to fade quickly away.

Desperate dreams live too short an hour.

You Are In My Life

You, on the stage of life the most recent act,
You, so close and so far,
You, who hide the color of your heart,
You, who deny my offering,
You, who restore forgotten landscapes,
You, who sound and laugh with me.

You, who can hurt with a syllable,
You are, finally,
Reluctant, in my life.

The poet with her companion Mario, Montalcino, Italy.

When Death

Suddenly, should take my breath away,
Raise a glass to celebrate
The many hours together,

Sing a little music to remember
Smiles,embraces given and received,
Break the silence, whistle softly in the wind,
Say my name, write an invisible epitaph
No one but you will understand.

An artisan, I'll leave behind
Pinned butterflies you can perhaps
Love, keep, classify or, bored, discard.

Have You Spun Your Web Today?

Sitting on a bench, old men
Gaze emptily beyond the tall trees,
Autumn leaves little hope
For the winter to come,
Crouching on their lives
They sing silent lullabies
To thoughts of the past and dream
Intoxicating alternatives:
Thin is the thread, difficult to weave...
Sitting on a bench, old men
Gaze emptily beyond the tall trees

Do Not Mourn

The horror of decay
The lack of warmth
The absence of touch
The dark, still silence
The immense humid cold
That death will bring...
Be afraid, instead, of the
Loss of memory and oblivion too
When each of us will be a name and two dates
In a registry of records,
When fingers will no longer remember
The skin they touched,
When eyes will no longer see
The beauty they saw,
When lips will no longer know
The softness they kissed.

Misers, we hoard
The riches of nothingness
In vain.

Condor

It binds your head
It devours your eyes
It tears at your mouth
It bleeds your heart

       White

It covers your arms
With warm sweat
It marks your body
With ravaging signs

       Red

Bend without defence
To its clawing embrace
Rejoice powerless
In its raptor wings
Listen to its anguished cries
Sinking in grey marbled cemeteries

Call its name shining within the light
Of the dark sun of deep memories...
When at the entrance
You see its shadow.
Run where it's darkest
Dream the sweetest song

Walk Over to the Far Away Side

Where the tide licks the earth
And abhorrent metamorphoses
Caress the dream that shapes the night,
Come to the window, look down into the valley,
Touch the shadow and dance in the circle.

Walk over to the far away side

There where Dali's landscape vomits
From obscene openings long strings of ants,
Where voracious eaters of flesh and dust, polluters of life,
Run with the blind mice who hold sacred emblems in their
                              mouths,
Enter carefully the space of time

Walk over to the far away side,
Cross into the mirror
Erase the future and look into your own eyes.

Vacuum

I wonder if the promise will be kept this time.

Open windows beckon...
Scarves of crimson
Draw arabesques in the air
Give life to vaporous forms.
Aerial bridges
Require acrobatic skills
For us to survive

Confiding to paper his latest ordeal,
Robie says — I write — I can't, I say,
I am dry — the well invaded by sand,
All shapes erased, all desires...
Noise outside, inside the head...

I am going deaf, she says.
I feel dizzy, very dizzy today
And I too am going deaf.
Remnants of lives are woven
Into fresh beginnings, over and over:
Can YOU repair the hanging threads,
The torn cloak, the worn cloth?
The weaver retired so long ago
Or was it yesterday.

Children play outside with a thousand loud cries,
They are so audibly alive
I feel I am going deaf — she says.

Closing Time

She stands naked in front of him
    She feels no shame
Light breaks through her body
    She senses no heat
Cold pierces her limbs
    She knows no pain
Darkness envelopes her face
    She sees no shadow

        And it means nothing.

Faint voices traverse empty chambers,
Gray walls crumble, fall,
Water fills the dry bed, swelling tides
Crush the rigor of the downward descent:
Subdued, conquered, she leans to the caress
— Slow, reluctant —

Dark hooves have cleared the way,
Flattened the pastures. She knocks at the door:
The grey-eyed wolf welcomes the hesitant guest,
Promises the magic of healing.
Incense spirals rise in the corner
Invoke sublime blessing
The wizard whispers his spell,
Calls the gathering to assemble,
The verdict is pronounced: slowly, she enters
The amorous waters, liquid tomb,
All enveloping, sweet, dark transparence

She sees no shadow
She knows no pain
She senses no heat
She feels no shame

        And it means nothing.

Mud dwellings at Matamata, Morocco.

Notes & Commentary

The first section of Napolitano's current volume *To Know the Desert* is taken verbatim from her section of the *Sextet One Anthology*, published by Pennywhistle Press in 1996. Her work was introduced by Pierre Saint-Amand who is Professor of French Studies and Comparative Literature at Brown University in Providence, Rhode Island. He is well-known in both the academic worlds of the United States and France for his literary criticism of Eighteenth Century French Literature; his keen analysis has revealed hitherto unsuspected shadows at the heart of the Enlightenment. His works have been published in both English and French. Recent publications include: *Le Lois de l'hostilité* (1992) and *The Libertine's Progress* (1994), as well as numerous books of literary criticism. The introduction follows:

EROS ON THE EDGE

Whoever said that poetry could not be intimate, even indiscreet — that it excluded from its domain anything but rigid abstraction — that it condemned words to cold and sterile thought? Annamaria Napolitano tells us quite the contrary. She writes at the very edge of emotion, in the immediacy of *affect,* in the intimacy of *pathos.*

We are drawn in by the indiscretion of her writing; we adopt it as our own. This poet bears witness to the emotions of our time (for epochs do indeed have their own emotions: solitude, the frenzy to love, the distance separating bodies, despair). In Annamaria's poetry, all of this culminates in an explosion of words, but within the contradictory discipline of poetry, the deliberate poverty of the poem. This is verse written on the verge of catastrophe, in the irreparability of lives and missed embraces.

Annamaria Napolitano presents an impossible choreography of bodies. Her poetry repeats an unbelievably missed connection. Her target is the site of an event that has not yet taken place, a perpetual failure, a coitus condemned to its own imaginative fabrication. This coitus is repeated in a plaintive echo that serves only to deepen the abyss, the absent element around which this poetry is built.

The miracle of this writing is that, in the archetypal boldness of *affect,* it aims at transparency and infinite comprehension. This is an open hermeneutics, one that ends up excluding thought, distancing it from word and body: *the mind erased.* In that sense, this poetry also categorically refuses interiority. It is no accident that, in the calculated conflation, "my soul my body," the poet points to the sensualist imperative: Napolitano's eros is above all tactile. Touch is the only sense present in this poetry textured with excrescences, with surfaces awaiting the hand's touch, the caress. It is a poetry of the skin, impregnated with secretions rather than secrets. The poet bleeds, weeps and screams and is utterly given over to the other, that absolute absence which compels sterile demand. This feeling crops up often in infinite demand: *desire unfulfilled.*

Yet it would be unjust to reduce Annamaria Napolitano's lyricism simply to the need for the other, or (and this amounts to the same thing) to the egotistical, obscene territory of the self. Exile (the poet's lament also turn toward her native Italy) and mourning (for father and husband) are both at the horizon of this poetry: as if genealogy were overwhelmed by the negative, as if all bonds already belonged to absence. From here this poetry opens onto a broader space: the echo of a higher thought, eternal emotions; hence its archaic force, the ancient voice added to the heavy, deadly present. To this dizzying unhappiness she gives the same name as all the great moderns: the apocalypse. And this is why her poetry speaks to us, *touches* us. It reminds us that the apocalypse is banal, hovering daily, close by our unhappiness, and that it ends up resonating in us, cosmically. The apocalypse is with us, now.

Translated from the French by Jennifer Curtiss Gage

A BRIDGE OF POETRY

Victor di Suvero

Poetry has a history of having a life of its own. Wherever it comes to life it speaks to its public in immediate terms and, as we all know, it also speaks through the centuries. From Homer to Dante to Shakespeare to Neruda, poetry transcends time and even the barriers of language to permit the sharing of thoughts, feelings, ideas and beliefs that become part of our human heritage.

The challenges that exist in the translation of poetry from one language into equivalent poetry in another are well known. The many versions of some of the most glorious poems continue to stir the hearts of successive generations. In time people all over the world have learned and continue to enjoy the Song of Solomon, the Inferno, Hamlet and the songs of Rumi. The translator often serves as the Bridge Builder for poetry.

In the case of the present work which does contain some translations, we have a rare example of a Poet expressing her native sensibility, shaped as it was in Fascist Italy in her youth, in English, her adopted and current language. The language of her life, her teaching and her writing is clear and fulfilled in itself. However, to really appreciate the work one must realize that most of the poetry is Italian in its concepts and sensibility even though expressed in English. The Poet becomes her own Bridge Builder. This applies not only to the expressions that she uses but also to the core concepts upon which she builds her poems.

The work can really be seen as a multicultural expression of feelings and their manifestation in the poems themselves. Looking at a landscape through tinted sunglasses gives the viewer a sight that does differ from the one seen by the naked eye. The poet's Italian origins give us Italian poetry in English, not as a translation, but as an unusual expression, of one language in another. By doing so the poet continues the Bridge Building which represents such an important aspect of her work.

Czes Milosz and Joseph Brodsky have met the same sort of challenge in their own ways. Annamaria Napolitano in this collection manages to express herself in an equivalent manner and is truly effective in providing the reader with a bicultural expression that is both brilliant and rewarding, building an effective bridge between her Italian sensibility and its English manifestation.

Inside the Certosa di San Martino, Naples, Italy.

A PERSONAL COMMENTARY

I consider poetry a subjective exercise that affords the reader possible points of personal identification, therefore, the photographs that punctuate this collection should be considered referential images to help envision the tangible reality beyond the mere word, be it in the past or in the present.

The metaphors — the deserts, the caravans, the river and the sea, are the background against which my life has taken shape, as is perhaps true also for those who have chosen to read my poetry.

It is my hope that in reading them — as it happens to me over and over again — one can

> *...sit, gaze, in silent wonder*
> *at the many lives I have lived,*
> *at the many lives I have witnessed!*

With my heartfelt thanks to Victor and Sunny, who helped this book become a reality.

ANNAMARIA